Michael Winicott

BUSINESS LESSONS FROM BILL GATES

Teachings from the richest man in the world

© 2015 by Michael Winicott.

© 2015 by UNITEXTO

Published by UNITEXTO

TABLE OF CONTENTS

WEALTH AND FAME ARE NOT ANSWERS TO LIFE,
LIVING FOR THE OTHERS IS!

CONCLUSION

Business Lessons from Bill Gates

1. Introduction

Thanks for taking the time to be here. In the next pages, you will take a journey that will show you the most important facts of the life of the genius Bill Gates. You will also see the best lessons we can extract from his unique experience.

Why do we write about Bill Gates?

Simply because this kind of leaders serve as great inspiration for others. We trust that this book will impact your life in the best way possible. Every dream is possible, and we believe that the best way to start a path to fulfilling yours is by learning what the great men in history have done.

Welcome to this amazing story!

2. Brief Summary of the Genius Life:

Starting with his childhood, Bill had shown signs of intelligence from the very beginning. Bill started his education in a public school but quickly lost all interest in what teachers had to offer. He was shifted to a private school called Lakeside, and that was probably the first step towards building this empire. Why? Because at Lakeside he met one of the loves of this life: the computer. It was a teletype computer donated by the Mothers Club. Bill became fascinated with the computer and the things it could do.

While he was attending School, he blossomed and flourished in every subject. He even excelled at drama and English. He was so good at mathematics that he was exempted from his math class to practice his programming hobby. It was also at Lakeside School that he met Paul Allen who was a computer enthusiast himself. Bill and Paul soon became really good friends and both spent lots of time together in the computer lab.

Gates had not yet graduated high school when he and Allen developed a program named "Traf-o-Data" and wanted to start a business of their own. But Bill's parents pushed him to complete school and attend college. So,he let go the business idea and went to Harvard after graduating from Lakeside in 1973. He joined Harvard as a pre-major law. People would usually find him in the computer lab instead of class. However, he was so intelligent that was able to pass all tests with good grades. Meanwhile, Paul Allen dropped out of his university and started working for

Honeywell. Bill and Paul read about an Altair computer in a magazine and were fascinated by the possibilities of what this computer could do. They called the company that was making it and offered to write software for them. In a period of two months, they wrote the code, Paul went to Albuquerque to test it, and it worked out fine. That code was named BASIC.

In 1975 Bill Gates dropped out of Harvard and he and his friend started Microsoft (Initially Micro-soft). After 3 years, Microsoft moved to Washington was able to make $2.5 million in revenues. Bill Gates was great at software development and as well as business operations. He personally read every line of every code that was developed. As more and more computer companies started to emerge, Bill was able to meet the CEO of IBM (International Business Machine) with the help of his mother. He signed a deal with IBM to provide for an operating system for their upcoming personal computer. Although Microsoft had not yet developed such an operating system, Gates bought a similar system from a third party and soon obtained its full rights. The software developer that sold Gates the operating system sued Microsoft for not telling him about the IBM deal. An out of court settlement was made and the issue was resolved.

The operating system named MS-DOS was sold to IBM but the source code was not given. That enabled Microsoft to get license fees and start growing at a very rapid pace. In 1983 Paul Allen was diagnosed with cancer. A year later he was treated fully and he was back to normal but he resigned from the company and went into other businesses. In 1985 Bill Gates launched Windows for the first time. The Windows Operating System was much similar to the operating system that was in the Apple's computers. Apple sued Microsoft for stealing the software but Microsoft was able to prevail in the courts.

In 1986, Bill Gates decided to take Microsoft public at an initial price of $21 per share. He retained 45% of the shares and soon became a millionaire. In 2001, Bill Gates wealth was estimated at $101 billion.

About his personal life, Bill first met Melinda (A Microsoft executive at the moment) in 1989 and was very impressed with her organizational skills. They soon developed a close relationship and got married in the beginning of 1994. In 1996, their first daughter was born: Jennifer Gates. After one year of Jennifer's birth, the Gates family moved to a 55,000 sq. feet home that was valued at $54 million.

In the year 2000, they formed the Bill and Melinda Gates Foundation. Since then, Bill Gates has been involved in a lot of philanthropic work. It was also in that year when he stepped down as the CEO Microsoft and started devoting more and more time to the Foundation. In 2014, Bill also resigned as Chairman of Microsoft and became "just" a technology adviser.

3. The 10 most important business lessons

3.1 Do what YOU want to do, not what others want you to do.

It was a very difficult time in the life of Bill Gates. His parents wanted him to be successful by taking a safe and standard career path that would guarantee a good future. For this reason, William and Mary Gates pushed Bill to study law at Harvard and become a successful lawyer just like his father. But he was young, energetic and passionate about computers. He had a very good business sense and wanted to take his chances in the newly emerging computer market.

Bill from the very beginning was a kid with great vision. As a teenager, he clearly viewed that computers would need good software to be useful. He realized this when he and his friend Paul Allen wrote the BASIC language for the Altair computer and found out that it was successful. Regardless of his passion for the computers, Bill's parents pushed him and sent him to Harvard as a pre-major law. It did not take Bill long to realize that he would not be a good law student no matter how hard he tried. The fire inside him was burning for the love of computers. He decided to take his chances and stepped into the computer industry with his friend Paul Allen.

Bill Gates' parents were not at all pleased but it was his mother that eased the tension. Finally his parents decided to stand behind what their son believed in.

Microsoft took off with a very shaky footing. The BASIC software that they developed for the Altair computer netted Microsoft $20,000 plus royalties. That amount could not even cover overhead expenditures. But Bill was determined to make Microsoft successful and he could envision that there would be a great need for good software. To make his dream come true, Bill Gates used to read every single line of code that was written in the initial years. With his hard work and great sense of business he was able to make Microsoft stable by the year 1978 with Microsoft annually grossing $2.5 million.

After that, Microsoft grew at a very rapid pace and soon they were establishing offices in other countries of the world including Great Britain and Japan. But the news of Paul Allen being diagnosed with cancer left everyone at Microsoft shocked and soon Paul resigned. With one of the founders gone, it was all on Bill to take the company further. But it was his love for the company and the passion that he had for computers that enabled him to keep on going. Similarly at many other stages of his life, such as the lawsuit by Apple or the investigations by the Federal Government, it was his passion and love that made Bill stand like a rock in front of any difficulty. If he had not loved what he did, he might have given up. But it was the inspiration he found in developing computer software that kept him going. Time proved that Bill Gates had made the right decision by pursuing his dreams.

3.2 Life is uncertain, take a chance!

There are many things we plan for ourselves. Starting from the tiniest of things like planning about our morning chores to the major decisions of life like marrying someone, we always make plans. However, things don´t need to work out the way we plan. Wise are those that adjust and adapt. Bill Gates was no stranger to uncertainty and many times he had to adapt to the environment around him. To achieve the highest levels of success, he knew that he would have to sometimes go with the flow and sometimes against it. But there was one thing that Bill was very clear about: sometimes in life we need jump to take a chance.

Gates had a very good business sense since his childhood. He would often come up with innovative ideas and excellent business strategies. From organizing and conducting the family athletic games in the summer to his first business venture at the age of 15, he consistently showed signs of being a successful businessman and a good entrepreneur. The first chance that he took was when he left high school to go into business with Paul Allen. Their program "traf-o-data" was quite successful and they netted a good amount from their software. But due to his parents' pressure Bill came back to high school. In 1973, after scoring a remarkable 1590 / 1600 in the SAT, he went to Harvard as a pre-major law as per the wish of his parents. But he could not quench his thirst for computers and was mostly found in the Harvard's computer lab.

Barely two years had passed in Harvard and Bill Gates was ready to start a new adventure with his school friend Paul. Paul told Bill about the new Altair computer that was coming out and they decided to write software for it. They spent two months in the Harvard computer lab and completed writing the BASIC software. When Paul Allen went to MITS to test the software, Bill Gates had made up his mind that if the software was successful, he and Paul would take a chance and start a company of their own. And the latter obviously ended up happening.

Bill Gates dropped out of Harvard in his junior year and took another chance with his life. He and Paul Allen established Microsoft in a room at Harvard. Similar to this, he took many other chances during the course of establishing Microsoft as the largest software company in the world. He took a chance when he bought software from Seattle Computer Products and sold it to IBM. Many say that it was morally not justified but nevertheless it was a huge risk that Bill took. This deal later on proved to be the first step towards a flourishing Microsoft. Taking calculated risks and taking chances at various points enabled Bill to experiment several things and learn from them. He always believed that when you venture into the unknown, you learn a lot no matter what. This certainly helped him achieve the heights he dreamed about as a teenager.

3.3 When the going gets tough, the tough gets going.

Most of us have heard this saying, but a very few among us have actually implemented it. Life is not always easy. It brings with it the good moments, the bad moments, the moments of happiness and the moments of sadness. That is how life is and the sooner we accept this fact, the better it is for us. Bill Gates learned it at a very young age that whenever you are under a difficult situation, you don't just sit down and mourn over it, you get up and do something. The first major test of the above saying came in Bill Gates' life when he was banned from using the school's computer on account of hacking. Bill at that age loved computer and he wanted to spend as much time with it as possible. He could have just abandoned his hobby at that time. But he was resolute to do something about it and he went on to be a tough cookie. He and his friend Paul Allen offered to debug the program of the computer company that provided them computer time. They also wrote a payroll program for the same company. Along with that, Bill wrote a program to sought students into classes. Due to their services the ban was lifted and he was able to use the computer once again.

This important lesson that Bill Gates learned, is one that would help him in his future life. The Microsoft's road to success was full of bumps and ditches. But from his very early years, Bill had learned to be tough during challenging times. Another test of his toughness came when he decided put all his energies to work at the newly found Microsoft and he dropped out of Harvard. Microsoft was established on a very shaky footing and no one was sure where this venture would lead to. Bill had to work 16 hours a day in the first few years of Microsoft. He personally had to read every line of code that was written to make sure that there were no errors. Sometimes, he even corrected codes that his employees wrote. This again was a very tough time for Microsoft and Bill Gates. But his determination and resolute nature stood firm against all the problems that he had to face.

Further in his life, he faced many difficult situations that required Gates to be tough. As the head of a company that was rising at a very rapid pace, Bill Gates had to sustain a lot of pressure. He had to face three major lawsuits, an investigation by the federal government for illegal business deals and another lawsuit that could have resulted in breaking up Microsoft into an operating systems company and a software company. The lawsuit by Seattle Computer Products could have been a turning point in history. But it was the intelligence and the unwavering nature of Bill Gates that kept Microsoft going under such demanding and testing circumstances. Another lawsuit by Apple was made to Microsoft in 1985 when Steve Jobs alleged that Microsoft had stolen his idea by launching Windows OS. Again these were testing times for Microsoft but Bill Gates was determined not to let Microsoft fail. In between all this, he had to deal with the death of his mother. Regardless of all these circumstances, Bill Gates stood firm against the wind of difficulties and problems. He knew that only the tough survive during testing times.

3.4 Believe in yourself, if you want others to believe in you.

The journey that started at Lakeside School with a teenager dreaming of changing the world through computers, ended with that teenager becoming the richest man of the world. The dream of Bill Gates that every home will have a computer with Microsoft software in it seems to be coming true with every passing day. When Bill discussed this idea with other people in those days, most of them did not believe it and said that it was a highly unlikely thing to happen. But Bill Gates believed in himself. He believed in his purpose and burned the midnight oil to make his dream come true.

When Bill started Microsoft after dropping out from Harvard, his parents were not at all impressed with him and they were angry with such a decision. But it was the belief in himself that convinced his parents that it was the right decision. If he had not believed in himself, he would not have achieved the remarkable feats that he was able to achieve throughout his life. Bill Gates had to pass not one but many such tests of self-belief in his journey.

It was in the year 1976 when he wrote a letter to all the computer hobbyists and condemned the habit of software sharing. All the computer hobbyists did not like his letter and his letter was received with hatred and revulsion. According to them this was a hindrance in the way of the development of the computers. But Bill Gates believed in himself and was keen to come up with a way to stop the software sharing. Finally in the year 1980, when Microsoft launched MS-DOS, they sold licenses for the number of copies that anyone wanted to buy. So if someone bought 100 licenses, they could only install MS-DOS on a 100 computers.

Bill Gates "paying for the software" idea had now begun to take shape. His determination and the willingness to believe in himself paved the way for his idea. Finally the world also agreed to his view and everyone started paying for software. On some other occasions too, his self-belief came in really handy and it helped him achieve great tasks that he otherwise might not have achieved. When Paul Allen left Microsoft after being diagnosed with cancer, it was the belief in himself that kept Bill Gates going. Also when Microsoft was lodged with allegations and Bill Gates was under immense pressure, it was the belief in himself that he was able to fight back. He stood firm against all such problems and emerged victorious. To establish an organization the size of Microsoft wasn't an easy task. If not for self-belief, Bill Gates would have given up to the problems and difficulties that he faced in making Microsoft what it is today. Self-belief really is an important virtue and has the power to overcome any difficulty that comes in your way. Bill Gates is a living example of this. He has taught all of us that belief in one's self is a virtue that each one of us should possess if we want to reach the heights of glory.

3.5 Love is what makes you complete.

Bill Gates was a very busy man especially during the early years of Microsoft. He had to work 16 hours a day and had a lot of burden on himself. He and Paul would sit together for hours to discuss the strategies they should use for marketing their products. Sometimes they would sit an entire day and night discussing an important piece of code that was causing some problems. They did not get up until and unless the problem at hand was solved. This was a routine and both of them were no strangers to working long hours. With such a busy schedule, Bill Gates barely had time to think about love. He was head over heels in love with Microsoft. Microsoft was his life and he had no time to think about anything else.

However when Microsoft established its footings in the software industry, it was then that Bill Gates started thinking about his love life. Like every man, he felt a void in his life and wanted to fill it as soon as possible. It was also because of the upbringing of his mother that he wanted a complete life where he had a family to cherish. He always idealized his mother and father and said in an interview that, "I want to have some of the magic too." He was referring to the amazing connection that his father and mother shared. It was in 1989 when Bill first met the raven haired, lively and organized Melinda French. A few months after their first meeting, Bill Gates saw her in the parking lot of Microsoft and asked her out.

This was the beginning of a new era for Bill. The couple kept on dating for a good amount of time and it wasn't until 1993 that Bill and Melinda decided to marry. When Bill Gates was asked about his marriage he said, "It has made me wiser and complete. I look at things in a different perspective now". Certainly the void that was there in the life of Bill Gates was filled by the love that Melinda had for the billionaire CEO of Microsoft. In 1994 Bill got married with Melinda in Hawaii. The 15-minute wedding was really expensive but why would Bill Gates think about money when he had billions of dollars at his expense. Bill Gates and Melinda French started their new life on 1st of January, 1994. But soon after their marriage, Bill's mother passed away. At this sad moment that engulfed Bill Gates with depression, Melinda was the one that helped Bill get back on track. She has certainly played a very important role in the life of Bill Gates.

Before he had fallen in love, Bill was incomplete. But Melinda French came into his life and filled that void extremely well. She always stood by Bill and supported him in every way. She made Bill a complete man and gave him a family he could love and spend quality time with. Melinda also encouraged him to devote his wealth to the problems of the world and as a result, today we see Bill and Melinda Gates Foundation working for the betterment of humanity. Melinda taught Bill how to love the world. Bill Gates' life was certainly completed with Melinda. It changed his perspective and made him a much better and complete person.

3.6 You will fail at some point in life; learn to fight back after the failure.

Bill Gates' success story has a lot of failures at different points of time. It is a famous quotation of Bill Gates that,

"Success is a lousy teacher. It seduces smart people into thinking they can't lose."

Bill Gates firmly believed that with every failure it comes a lesson. If you are learning from the lesson that failure taught you and you are improving yourself as a result, you are on the right track. In his story of establishing Microsoft, he had to face a lot of failures but every time he failed, he got up and made himself better. This was an excellent approach as the new venture brought with it all sorts of difficulties and problems. He knew that he will fail at some points but the failure will not mean that everything was over. He always took failure as a challenge and he would not sit with comfort until and unless he overcame that challenge.

When Bill Gates dropped out of Harvard and started his own business, many thought that he will fail and he will not be able to make a successful business out of it. Even the father of Bill Gates, William H. Gates II thought that that Bill wasn't going to succeed. He was angry with Bill upon his decision of leaving Harvard for starting Microsoft. Many thought that it was a failure of Bill Gates and he had not made a good decision. But he was determined and he knew that with determination he can overcome all the odds. He started working day and night for his new venture to be successful. When Bill announced the Windows Operating System, he did not have any product in his hand at that time. It was only a bluff just to stay in competition with Apple who had promised its users a graphical interface. Bill Gates knew that he could fail to deliver the promised product but he took a chance.

When Microsoft was developing Windows OS it faced a lot of problems and they could not somehow compile the complete code of the visual interface of the operating system. However, Bill Gates knew what Apple was launching on their computer because Microsoft had worked with Apple to make their version of the operating system. Bill Gates taking advantage of Apple not licensing their product, took their code and wrote his code all over again with each function distinctly different from Apple's operating system code. He had once failed but he had not given up. He had a very good and keen business sense and that enabled him to take advantage of the situation. He had not done anything wrong legally as he proved in the later years by averting the lawsuit Apple had launched on Microsoft. Bill Gates once again proved that he was a tough cookie and to him failure was just another challenge.

Along the road to success many bumps and ditches were faced by Bill Gates and his team. But they were determined not to back down against any challenge. This skill helped him motivate his employees and himself. He did not back down at any point and always kept going no matter how difficult the circumstances were. To him failure was a good teacher and he learned a lot from failing at different times in life. But he made sure that every time he fails, he works harder and harder next time.

3.7 Everything that happens in life is not in your control, but you yourself are.

Bill Gates is a human just like us. Maybe a little more intelligent than an average person but nevertheless he is a human being, with normal feelings and emotions. He also felt sad and depressed in the times of severe tension. Many times in his life he had to deal with such situations. He had to go through everything an average human goes through and maybe more than that. There were times when he couldn't sleep because of all the pressures he had to sustain. But from the early few lessons, Bill Gates had learned that everything that happens in our lives is not in our control, however we ourselves are. This was a very important lesson that helped him get through a lot of testing times throughout his life. Let's see a few examples and see how he dealt with them.

In 1970, Bill Gates and Paul Allen decided to go into business together with their "traf-o-data" but because of his parents' pressure, Bill had to go back to school. He kept his cool at that moment and Paul and Bill decided that they will give it another shot later in the life. In 1973, Bill graduated from the Lakeside school. He scored 1590 out of 1600 in the SAT and went to Harvard as a pre-major law. This was not at all something Bill Gates wanted. It was the turn of events that landed him in Harvard and as a pre-major law too. But Bill Gates did not lose control and kept on chasing his dream of opening a software house. He spent most of his time in Harvard's computer lab and practiced computer programming. Over the period of two years, Bill Gates was much more accomplished in programming than he was before and now he was ready to take a leap of faith.

In his junior year, he left Harvard and decided to open a company named "Micro-soft" with Paul Allen. The hyphen was soon dropped and the name was changed to "Microsoft". Microsoft was very shaky in the beginning. Bill Gates and Paul Allen had to work really hard to establish its footings in the software industry. They worked day and night to make their venture successful. A few years after the establishment of Microsoft, they were sued by Seattle Computer

Products. It was a testing time for Bill Gates and the newly established Microsoft but Bill Gates knew that he had to remain calm. He figured out a solution and made an out of court settlement with the Seattle Company. Similarly in the lawsuit launched by Apple in 1985, Bill Gates kept everything under his control.

No matter what the situation, Bill Gates made sure that he kept his cool. He knew that everything in life will not turn out to be exactly as planned. But to deal with anything that was unplanned Bill Gates was always prepared. He was very close to his mother and when she passed away in 1994, he was devastated and broken. It was the first time in life when he felt lost. But it was his wife Melinda who supported him and made him look at life in a new perspective. With this incident, Bill Gates had reaffirmed his lesson that everything in life is not in your control, but you yourself are! He knew that he has to keep on going and this is exactly what he did.

3.8 A good life partner can make a lot of difference.

Bill Gates got married at the age of 37. It was pretty late according to normal standards. But considering the fact that he had such a busy life with Microsoft, maybe it wasn't too late. It was in 1989 when he first met

Melinda French at a press event in New York. Melinda French was a Microsoft executive then who had recently joined the company. She was a smart and organized person and she graduated from Duke University with a degree in computer science and economics. It was many months after their first meeting in New York that Bill Gates met Melinda in the parking lot of Microsoft. This is where he asked Melinda out. She was a little surprised but she said yes. When asked about why she said yes, she commented "*He was funnier than I expected him to be*". Bill Gates and funny, now who would have thought of that?

Over the period of three years the couple found an intimate touch to their relationship. Their relationship kept on growing and both decided to get married. It was in the year 1993 when Bill Gates proposed Melinda French by diverting a chartered plane to Omaha. Warren Buffet, who is a close friend of Bill Gates, helped him pick out a ring for Melinda. Bill Gates' mother was diagnosed with breast cancer in the same year. Bill Gates was depressed and sad but he wanted to give his mother happiness by getting married while she was alive. On 1st of January in the year 1994, Bill and Melinda got married on an island in Hawaii. The wedding was short but expensive and more important than that, Bill Gates had found a really good partner in the form of Melinda. She was smart, business savvy and a very organized person. This was exactly what Bill Gates needed.

A few months after marriage, his mother Mary Maxwell died. Bill Gates was broken and shattered. It was the first time he was feeling completely lost. Bill Gates wife Melinda French decided that Bill should get a fresh perspective on life and she decided that the couple should go on a world tour. They travelled around the world and visited many places. It was during this travelling that Bill and Melinda Gates saw that the world needed someone who could work for the better. Melinda convinced Bill to form a foundation that could work on world health and education. As a result William H. Gates Foundation came into existence in 1994. Melinda French helped Bill Gates through this difficult phase of life and Bill Gates was up and running once again.

Further in life, Melinda Gates played a very vital role in the life of Bill. Two years after their marriage, Melinda and Bill Gates were gifted with a daughter. Melinda gave good quality time to her family and made sure that Bill did not have any problems from her side. After the formation of Bill and Melinda Gates Foundation in the year 2000, she started giving 30 hours per week to the foundation as well. All the family foundations were combined under this name and world poverty was made a priority focus. Melinda Gates proved that behind a successful man there is a perfect woman by advising Bill on important issues and giving him support when he needed it the most. Bill Gates is not shy of praising her wife and he says that a good partner in life does make a difference.

3.9 You cannot make this world a perfect place, but it's worth trying.

The world is not perfect and so is the case with the human beings living in it. Bill Gates was not perfect throughout his life but let's say that he was better than the most. Bill Gates' mother Mary always believed that, "To whom much is given, much is expected". Mary Maxwell always took part in charity events and was always on the front foot to help people in any way she could. She also took Bill Gates to such events and this inculcated a spirit of living for the others on him. Bill, like his mother, donated money to charity and always believed that everyone can contribute to the best of this world regardless of their social position. Bill Gates' mother always encouraged Bill to take part in charities. She herself was a role model to Bill and he made sure that he filled his mother's shoes in a perfect manner by working for the world.

Bill Gates estimated net worth at the moment is around 70 billion dollars and he has decided to give most of this wealth to the Bill and Melinda Gates Foundation. The couple has already donated more than 40 billion to the foundation. Warren Buffet who is a good friend of Bill Gates and a billionaire himself also gave a considerable amount to the Bill and Melinda Gates Foundation. In a press conference, Bill Gates told the media that he would leave his three children with 10 million dollars each. All the remaining wealth would shall be used for the betterment of the world. Bill and Melinda Gates Foundation is doing a tremendous job helping the poor. They launch vaccine campaigns, health campaigns and education campaigns throughout the world. They mainly target those countries of the world where there is a lot of poverty and people do not have money to buy medicines and other basic necessities of life.

When Bill Gates was asked about how much will he be able to change the world, he answered by saying that he cannot make this world perfect, however he can play his part in making this world a better place and is always worth trying. That was a very positive notion to everyone that was listening. In a way, he encouraged each and everyone to play their respective roles in making this world better. He also encourages the wealthy to spend their money for the betterment of this world. A lot of this thought pattern has to do with Bill's mother and a lot more has to do with Melinda. Melinda Gates is the one who encouraged Bill Gates to do philanthropic work throughout the world. And we certainly see her influence.

Bill and Melinda Gates Foundation primary focus is education, healthcare and fighting poverty. The foundation donates at least 5% of its total assets to the charitable works in order to keep the charity going. The foundation currently has assets in British Petroleum, Coca Cola Inc., Mc. Donald's Corp., Wal-Mart and many other notable firms. Bill, Melinda and Irish musician Bono were named Persons of the year by Time magazine in the year 2005. That happened because of the charitable works done by them. Bill Gates has taught us that no matter how small our contribution towards making this world a better place, it is always worth it. He has presented himself as a role model for the rest of the world. Melinda Gates role in this regard is also noteworthy and she has to be given credit for all that she has done over the years. The couple truly is a role model for the rest of the world.

3.10 Wealth and fame are not answers to life, living for the others is!

Bill Gates was named the richest person of the world for 13 consecutive years by Forbes until he was surpassed by his friend Warren Buffet. He has had so much wealth and fame that anyone can dream of. Being at the top of the world at such a young age is not easy and neither is staying there for a long period of time. But Bill Gates has done both the things. His life is a role model to many and many look up to him. The wealth that Bill Gates has is so much that his generations to come can sit, relax and eat. But Bill Gates has shown that he is great by not falling in love with his wealth and fame. He has taught us that these two things are not the answers to this life.

Wealth and fame are two things that most of the people in this world crave for and work had for. A man who got so much of both says that these two things are not the answers to life with the help of his actions. He has given so much to his community and has been bestowed with many awards and honors. But the awards and honors are not the reasons Bill Gates does this philanthropic work; it is solely for the reason of making the world a better place. This characteristic in Bill Gates is much owed to his mother who herself was very active in civic affairs and took part in charity events. She always took young Bill with her and he not only had a close relationship with his mother but he also idealized her. After his mother passed away, Bill Gates made sure that he filled the shoes of his mother by doing charity and by helping humanity.

Melinda Gates also had a very helping and generous nature. After she came into Bill Gates' life she also encouraged him to continue his philanthropic efforts. She herself wanted to work for the betterment of humanity and she joined hands with Bill Gates to help make this world a better place. She worked under the umbrella of William H. Gates Foundation as well but then the primary focus was education and health. Later on when Bill and Melinda Gates Foundation was created, they shifted their focus towards eliminating poverty. Bill Gates in the year 1994 read the lives of the two great men that played an important part in the America's Industrial Revolution. It was then that he got inspired from the philanthropic works of Andrew Carnegie and John D. Rockefeller.

Bill Gates has surely taught us that wealth and fame are not answers to life. These two things may give you material comfort in the world but it is living for the others that gives one the peace of mind and heart. Bill

Gates has seen so much wealth and fame in his life that maximum population of the world can only dream of. When a statement such as this, "Living for the others is the actual purpose of life" comes from a man who has seen both wealth and fame so closely, then surely he is a man to be believed. Bill Gates and Melinda Gates are day-by-day contributing more and more to this world. He is an example for all the wealthy people in the world and also for the people who are not so wealthy. He believes that if everyone plays his part, big or small, then world will became a much better place.

4. Conclusion

The story of Bill Gates is a lesson for all of us. His inspiring story is not a single lesson but it is a collection of lessons that he taught us over the period of his life. The story started with a young boy imagining of a place where every home would have a computer and every computer would have software made by him. To many people that dream seemed impossible and far-fetched, but not to the determined and visionary Bill Gates. He was helped along his way by many people. He made a lot of friends during his journey of life, and also a few enemies. His story is inspiring and a lesson for all of us. Each chapter of his story holds a lesson for all the people around the world, a lesson worth listening to and a lesson from which we should learn from. The lessons that we discussed in this book were some of the many important lessons that Bill Gates' life taught us.

As a young boy, Bill Gates was a very determined and intelligent boy. At a young age of 12 years, he read the complete encyclopedia. He was popular in school as a nerd. It is a fact that he still acknowledges and one that he is proud of. Once Bill Gates said,

"Be nice to nerds. Chances are you will end up working for one someday."

When he was shifted to Lakeside school, which was a rigorous private preparatory school, Bill Gates was polished and nurtured into a smart young boy. It was there that he met the passion of his life, computer! Not only did he find computers, but also met a good friend Paul Allen at Lakeside school who co-founded Microsoft. As Bill was once recalled the time he spent at Lakeside school he commented that, "It was a golden time. All I cared about was computers." Further in a funny mood he said, "Now I am more concerned about my business". The funny side of Bill Gates is one that only few people saw. But the ones closest to him say that he is a pretty funny man.

When he founded Microsoft at the young age of 21 with his school friend Paul Allen, he taught the world that anyone could achieve greatness in the world. But it needs a lot of hard work, commitment, passion and a little bit of luck as well. Bill always believed that the hard work never lets you down and you always get rewarded sooner or later. Microsoft needed a lot of hard work and commitment in the beginning and Bill Gates made sure that he gave his all to the new company. With years of hard work put into Microsoft, he was able to make Microsoft the biggest software company on the planet. He faced a lot of difficulties in making Microsoft a success, but he stood firm against each problem and taught us that with determination you can emerge victorious in every battle of life. Bill Gates' mother and father encouraged him to be competitive from a very young age and that also helped him in his later life. Bill's mother was a very outgoing lady and a very generous one too. In the wedding shower of his wife Melinda, Mary Maxwell advised the couple to do charitable work and give back to the world in every way they can.

Bill Gates life was not all about work. He also had a soft side to him that a very few people knew about. When his friend Paul Allen was diagnosed with Hodgkin's disease, he became very sad and depressed. Also when Bill Gates got to know about his mother's cancer, he was devastated and broken. But in all the situations we see that Bill Gates did not give up and stood up every time the life gave him a blow. When Bill and Melinda started the William H. Gates Foundation in 1994, Bill told everyone that it was her mother and now her wife who had encouraged him to invest his money in the betterment of the world. According to him he had found a new perspective to life. The new perspective was that to live for the others is actual living. He was also inspired from the philanthropic works of Carnegie and Rockefeller. Since then he has always kept himself busy with the philanthropic work his foundation does all around the world. Melinda Gates has also played her part in Bill Gates' life. According to the Microsoft Billionaire, his partner for life Melinda made him look at life with a different purpose and now he feels like a wiser and a more complete man. To get a good partner in life is also a blessing and nature certainly gave Bill Gates the perfect partner in the form of Melinda French.

The boy, who started out as an ambitious young man looking to change the world with his crazy ideas, is now at a place where he can be proud of. The journey has not ended yet and Bill Gates still amazes the world with the wonderful things he still does. His most recent efforts in philanthropy are recognized and praised by everyone around the world. Bill Gates said that he is hopeful that one day this world will be a better place to live in. He believes that if all of us play our part, the day is not far when we shall achieve the goal of eradicating poverty from this world. Bill and Melinda Gates now live on a 55,000 sq. ft. home, which mostly serves as a business center. He has three children and enjoys a comfortable and happy life with his family. Bill Gates life is a lesson, a story worth reading and a story worth learning from.

BOOKS FROM MICHAEL WINICOTT

Another titles by Michael Winicott you may find interesting:

BRAIN: EXERCISES TO EMPOWER

BUSINESS PLAN: A practical guide

FACEBOOK MARKETING: Business Lessons from Mark Zuckerberg

HABITS: MICRO CHANGES for MACRO RESULTS

HENRY FORD: ENTERPRENEURSHIP LESSONS

JESUS: LEADERSHIP LESSONS

LEONARDO DA VINCI: CREATIVITY LESSONS

MARTIN LUTHER KING: LIFE LESSONS

OPRAH WINFREY: LIFE LESSONS

STEVE JOBS: BUSINESS LESSONS

WALT DISNEY: CREATIVITY LESSONS

WINSTON CHURCHILL: LEADERSHIP LESSONS

DID YOU ENJOY THIS BOOK?

Thanks for purchasing and reading this book. If you reached this page you had probably enjoyed it . Would you care to leave a positive review in Amazon?

This is very important for 2 reasons:

a) I need your feedback to improve the quality of my books

b) Other people may read and benefit from this book if you share your thoughts.

Thanks a lot!

Michael Winicott